knock
knock
Jokes

knock knock Jokes

Capella

This edition published in 2008 by Arcturus Publishing Limited
26/27 Bickels Yard, 151–153 Bermondsey Street,
London SE1 3HA

ISBN: 978-1-84193-779-3

Printed in China

Knock, knock...
Who's there?
Aliens...
Aliens who?
Just how many aliens do you know?

Knock, knock...
Who's there?
Phil...
Phil who?
Phil this bag with
money, I'm a robber!

Knock, knock...
Who's there?
Giraffe...
Giraffe who?
Giraffe to sit in front of me?

☺☺☺☺☺  ☺☺☺☺☺

Knock, knock...
Who's there?
Superman...
Superman who?
You know I can't reveal my secret identity!

Knock, knock...
Who's there?
Albert...
Albert who?
Albert you don't know who this is!

Knock, knock...
Who's there?
Carrie...
Carrie who?
Carrie the
bags into the
house please!

Knock, knock...
Who's there?
Alec...
Alec who?
Alec my lolly!

☺☺☺☺☺ ☺☺☺☺☺

Knock, knock...
Who's there?
Castro...
Castro who?
Castro bread upon
the waters!

Knock, knock...
Who's there?
Cash...
Cash who?
I knew you were nuts!

Knock, knock...
Who's there?
Cass...
Cass who?
Cass more flies with honey than vinegar!

Knock, knock...
Who's there?
Carl...
Carl who?
Carl get you there quicker
than if you walk!

Knock, knock...
Who's there?
Carmen...
Carmen who?
Carmen get it!

Knock, knock...
Who's there?
Jim...
Jim who?
Jim mind if I stay here tonight?

Knock, knock...
Who's there?
Frank...
Frank who?
Frankenstein!

Hi, I'm Frank

Knock, knock...
Who's there?
Oman...
Oman who?
Oman, you are cute!

Knock, knock...
Who's there?
Alec...
Alec who?
Alec-tricity. Isn't
that a shock!

Knock, knock...
Who's there?
Avenue...
Avenue who?
Avenue guessed yet?

Knock, knock...
Who's there?
Snow...
Snow who?
Snow use – I can't remember!

Knock, knock...
Who's there?
Donkey...
Donkey who?
Donkey Hotey!

Knock, knock...
Who's there?
Donna...
Donna who?
Donna sit under an apple tree
with anyone but me...!

Knock, knock...
Who's there?
Alex...
Alex who?
Alex the questions round here!

Knock, knock...
Who's there?
Cathy...
Cathy who?
Cathy the
doorbell, it's too
dark out
here!

Knock, knock...
Who's there?
Boo...
Boo who?
Don't get upset, it's only a game!

Knock, knock...
Who's there?
Atilla...
Atilla who?
Atilla you open this door I'm a gonna stand here!

Knock, knock...
Who's there?
Cassie...
Cassie who?
Cassie the forest for the trees!

Knock, knock...
Who's there?
Castor...
Castor who?
Castorblanca!

Knock, knock...
Who's there?
Little old lady...
Little old lady who?
Your yodelling's getting much better!

Knock, knock...
Who's there?
McKee...
McKee who?
McKee doesn't fit!

Knock, knock...
Who's there?
Celery...
Celery who?
Celery me your lunch will you, I'm hungry!

Knock, knock...
Who's there?
Celeste...
Celeste who?
Celeste time I'm going to tell you this!

Knock, knock...
Who's there?
Amahl...
Amahl who?
Amahl shook up!

Knock, knock...
Who's there?
China...
China who?
China just like old times isn't it!

Knock, knock...
Who's there?
Cecil...
Cecil who?
Cecil have music wherever she goes...!

Knock, knock...
Who's there?
Cecile...
Cecile who?
Cecile this envelope!

Knock, knock...
Who's there?
Pecan...
Pecan who?
Pecan somebody your own size!

☺☺☺☺☺ ☺☺☺☺☺

Knock, knock...
Who's there?
Douglas...
Douglas who?
Douglas is broken!

Knock, knock...
Who's there?
Alma...
Alma who?
Alma time seems to be spent on this doorstep!

Knock, knock...
Who's there?
Wanda...
Wanda who?
Wanda know how much
longer you're going to
keep me hanging
around out here!

Knock, knock...
Who's there?
Zone...
Zone who?
Zone shadow scares him!

Knock, knock...
Who's there?
Dotty...
Dotty who?
Dotty way the cookie crumbles!

Knock, knock...
Who's there?
Justin...
Justin who?
Justin time to let me in!

☺☺☺☺☺  ☺☺☺☺☺

Knock, knock...
Who's there?
Josie...
Josie who?
Josie anyone else out here?

Knock, knock...
Who's there?
Dummy...
Dummy who?
Dummy a favour and go away!

☺☺☺☺☺ ☺☺☺☺☺

Knock, knock...
Who's there?
Dunce...
Dunce who?
Dunce-ay another word!

Knock, knock...
Who's there?
Ooze...
Ooze who?
Ooze in charge round here!

☺ ☺ ☺ ☺ ☺  ☺ ☺ ☺ ☺ ☺

Knock, knock...
Who's there?
Alli...
Alli who?
Alligator, that's
who!

Knock, knock...
Who's there?
Matt...
Matt who?
Matt as well settle
down, looks like I'm
in for a long wait!

☺☺☺☺☺ ☺☺☺☺☺

Knock, knock...
Who's there?
Chas...
Chas who?
Chas pass the key through
the letter box and I'll open
the door myself!

Knock, knock...
Who's there?
Donatello...
Donatello who?
Donatello'n me!

Knock, knock...
Who's there?
Don Giovanni...
Don Giovanni who?
Don Giovanni talk to me?

Knock, knock...
Who's there?
Paul...
Paul who?
Paul the door open for goodness sake!

Knock, knock...
Who's there?
Woody...
Woody who?
Woody open the door if we asked him nicely?

Knock, knock...
Who's there
Zeb...
Zeb who?
Zeb better be a good reason for keeping me
waiting out here!

Knock, knock...
Who's there?
Polly...
Polly who?
Polly door handle
again, I think
it's just stiff!

Knock, knock...
Who's there?
Alvin...
Alvin who?
Alvin your heart - just you vait and see!

Knock, knock...
Who's there?
Candy...
Candy who?
Candy owner of this big red car come and move it off my drive!

Knock, knock...
Who's there?
Khan...
Khan who?
Khan you give me a lift to school?

Knock, knock...
Who's there?
Colin...
Colin who?
Colin in for a chat!

Knock, knock...
Who's there?
Alfred...
Alfred who?
Alfred of the dark!

☺☺☺☺☺ ☺☺☺☺☺

Knock, knock...
Who's there?
Chad...
Chad who?
Chad to make your
acquaintance!

Knock, knock...
Who's there?
Chip...
Chip who?
Chip of Fools!

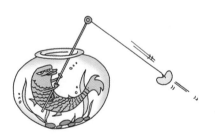

Knock, knock...
Who's there?
Bean...
Bean who?
**Bean fishing
lately?**

Knock, knock...
Who's there?
Dragon...
Dragon who?
Dragon your feet again!

☺☺☺☺☺ ☺☺☺☺☺

Knock, knock...
Who's there?
Europe...
Europe who?
Europe to no good!

Knock, knock...
Who's there?
Cologne...
Cologne who?
Cologne me names won't help!

Knock, knock...
Who's there?
Coolidge...
Coolidge who?
Coolidge a cucumber!

Knock, knock...
Who's there?
Kent...
Kent who?
Kent you stop asking questions
and open the door!

☺☺☺☺☺  ☺☺☺☺☺

Knock, knock...
Who's there?
Ahmed...
Ahmed who?
Ahmed a big mistake coming here!

I know kung fu...
I know kung fu who?
I'd better not upset you then!

Knock, knock...
Who's there?
Cohen...
Cohen who?
Cohen to knock just once more, then I'm going away!

Knock, knock...
Who's there?
Paula...
Paula who?
Paula up the door handle will you
and let me in!

☺☺☺☺☺ ☺☺☺☺☺

Knock, knock...
Who's there?
Daryl...
Daryl who?
Daryl never be
another you...!

Knock, knock...
Who's there?
Cher...
Cher who?
Cher and share alike!

Knock, knock...
Who's there?
Cherry...
Cherry who?
Cherry oh, see you later!

Knock, knock...
Who's there?
Esther...
Esther who?
Esther anything I can do for you?

Knock, knock...
Who's there?
Europe...
Europe who?
Europe'ning the door too slow, come on!

Knock, knock...
Who's there?
Dwayne...
Dwayne who?
Dwayne in Spain falls mainly on the plain...!

Knock, knock...
Who's there?
Ahmed...
Ahmed who?
Ahmed another
mistake!

Knock, knock...
Who's there?
Polly...
Polly who?
Polly door handle again,
I think it's just stiff!

Knock, knock...
Who's there?
Elias...
Elias who?
Elias a terrible thing!

Knock, knock...
Who's there?
Chester...
Chester who?
Chester the nick of time!

Knock, knock...
Who's there?
Chesterfield...
Chesterfield who?
Chesterfield my leg so I slapped him!

Knock, knock...
Who's there?
Opera...
Opera who?
Opera-tunity, and you thought
opportunity only knocked once!

Knock, knock...
Who's there?
Chuck...
Chuck who?
Chuck and see if the door is locked!

Knock, knock...
Who's there?
Amazon...
Amazon who?
Amazon of a gun!

Knock, knock...
Who's there?
Clara...
Clara who?
Clara space on
the table!

Knock, knock...
Who's there?
Enid...
Enid who?
Enid some more pocket money!

Knock, knock...
Who's there?
Diploma...
Diploma who?
Diploma to fix the leak!

Knock, knock...
Who's there?
Osborn...
Osborn who?
Osborn today – it's my birthday!

Knock, knock...
Who's there?
Cicero...
Cicero who?
Cicero the boat ashore!

Knock, knock...
Who's there?
Arnie...
Arnie who?
Arnie ever going to let me in?

☺☺☺☺☺  ☺☺☺☺☺

Knock, knock...
Who's there?
Ken...
Ken who?
Ken you come out to play?

Knock, knock...
Who's there?
Isabelle...
Isabelle who?
Isabelle not working?

Knock, knock...
Who's there?
Amos...
Amos who?
**Amos-quito is
chasing me - please
let me in!**

Knock, knock...
Who's there?
Colleen...
Colleen who?
Colleen up this mess!

Knock, knock...
Who's there?
Ammonia...
Ammonia who?
Ammonia little kid!

Knock, knock...
Who's there?
Parton...
Parton who?
Parton my French!

Knock, knock...
Who's there?
Cozy...
Cozy who?
Cozy who's knocking!

Knock, knock...
Who's there?
Evan...
Evan who?
Evan and earth!

Knock, knock...
Who's there?
Ezra...
Ezra who?
Ezra no hope for me?

Knock, knock...
Who's there?
Colin...
Colin who?
Colin the doctor, I feel ill!

Knock, knock...
Who's there?
Paris...
Paris who?
Paris the thought!

Knock, knock...
Who's there?
Gin...
Gin who?
Gin know how cold it is out here?

☺☺☺☺☺☺ ☺☺☺☺☺

Knock, knock...
Who's there?
Linda...
Linda who?
Linda hand to get
this heavy suitcase
up the steps!

Knock, knock...
Who's there?
Major...
Major who?
Major mind up to open the door yet?

Knock, knock...
Who's there?
Mandy...
Mandy who?
Mandy lifeboats!

Knock, knock...
Who's there?
Pasture...
Pasture who?
Pasture bedtime isn't it!

Knock, knock...
Who's there?
Pat...
Pat who?
Pat yourself on the back!

Knock, knock...
Who's there?
Dozen...
Dozen who?
Dozen anyone ever answer the door!

☺☺☺☺☺  ☺☺☺☺☺

Knock, knock...
Who's there?
Enoch...
Enoch who?
Enoch and Enoch
but no one answers
the door!

Knock, knock...
Who's there?
Ella...
Ella who?
Ella-vator. Doesn't that give you a lift!

☺☺☺☺☺ ☺☺☺☺☺

Knock, knock...
Who's there?
Dimitri...
Dimitri who?
Dimitri is where the
burgers grow!

Knock, knock...
Who's there?
Falafel...
Falafel who?
Falafel off my bike and cut my knee!

Knock, knock...
Who's there?
Ferdie...
Ferdie who?
Ferdie last time, open this door!

Knock, knock...
Who's there?
Tex...
Tex who?
Tex you ages to open the door!

☺☺☺☺☺  ☺☺☺☺☺

Knock, knock...
Who's there?
Yul...
Yul who?
Yul soon see!

Knock, knock...
Who's there?
Giraffe...
Giraffe who?
Giraffe to ask me that stupid question?

Knock, knock...
Who's there?
Mike...
Mike who?
Mike your
mind up!

Knock, knock...
Who's there?
Donald...
Donald who?
Donald come baby, cradle and all...!

Knock, knock...
Who's there?
Congo...
Congo who?
Congo out, I'm grounded!

Knock, knock...
Who's there?
Delhi...
Delhi who?
Delhicatessen!

Knock, knock...
Who's there?
Peg...
Peg who?
Peg your pardon, I've got the wrong door!

Knock, knock...
Who's there?
Gandhi...
Gandhi who?
Gandhi cane!

Knock, knock...
Who's there?
Germany...
Germany who?
Germany people knock
on your door?

Knock, knock...
Who's there?
Cook...
Cook who?
Cuckoo yourself, I don't come here
to be insulted!

Knock, knock...
Who's there?
Passion...
Passion who?
Passion through
and I thought
I'd say hello!

Knock, knock...
Who's there?
Darren...
Darren who?
Darren young man in his flying machine!

☺☺☺☺☺ ☺☺☺☺☺

Knock, knock...
Who's there?
Paul...
Paul who?
Paul up a chair and
I'll tell you!

Knock, knock...
Who's there?
Handel...
Handel who?
Handel with care!

Knock, knock...
Who's there?
Hank...
Hank who?
Hank you!

 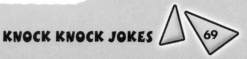

Knock, knock...
Who's there?
Police...
Police who?
Police let me in, I'm freezing out here!

Knock, knock...
Who's there?
Mike...
Mike who?
Mike car won't start, can I come in
and use the phone?

Knock, knock...
Who's there?
Teacher...
Teacher who?
Teacher self for a few days, I'm off on holiday!

Knock, knock...
Who's there?
Mouse...
Mouse who?
Mouse get a key
of my own!

Knock, knock...
Who's there?
Custer...
Custer who?
Custer penny to find out!

Knock, knock...
Who's there?
Arnold...
Arnold who?
Arnold friend you
haven't seen for years!

Knock, knock...
Who's there?
Cy...
Cy who?
Cy'n on the botton line!

Knock, knock...
Who's there?
Cyril...
Cyril who?
Cyril nice to meet you!

Knock, knock...
Who's there?
Handsome...
Handsome who?
Handsome chips through the keyhole
and I'll tell you more!

☺☺☺☺☺ ☺☺☺☺☺

Knock, knock...
Who's there?
Ford...
Ford who?
Ford he's a
jolly good fellow!

Knock, knock...
Who's there?
Josie...
Josie who?
Josie any reason to keep me
waiting out here!

Knock, knock...
Who's there?
Zeke...
Zeke who?
Zeke and you will find out!

Knock, knock...
Who's there?
Desiree...
Desiree who?
Desiree a ray of sunshine in my life...!

☺☺☺☺☺ ☺☺☺☺☺

Knock, knock...
Who's there?
Cereal...
Cereal who?
Cereal pleasure to
meet you!

Knock, knock...
Who's there?
Harmon...
Harmon who?
Harmon on your side!

Knock, knock...
Who's there?
Harold...
Harold who?
Harold are you?

Knock, knock...
Who's there?
Daisy...
Daisy who?
Daisy plays, nights he sleeps!

Knock, knock...
Who's there?
Dale...
Dale who?
Dale come if you ask dem!

Knock, knock...
Who's there?
Conga...
Conga who?
Conga on meeting like this!

Knock, knock...
Who's there?
Amory...
Amory who?
Amory Christmas!

Knock, knock...
Who's there?
Hannah...
Hannah who?
Hannah partridge in a pear tree!

Knock, knock...
Who's there?
Ivan...
Ivan who?
Ivan enormous snake
in my pouch!

Knock, knock...
Who's there?
India...
India who?
India is some of my stuff,
and I've come to collect it!

Knock, knock...
Who's there?
Chuck...
Chuck who?
Chuck the key under the door
and I'll let myself in!

Knock, knock...
Who's there?
Harry...
Harry who?
Harry up and answer this door!

Knock, knock...
Who's there?
Havanna...
Havanna who?
Havanna a wonderful time,
wish you were here!

Knock, knock...
Who's there?
De Niro...
De Niro who?
De Niro I am to you, the more I like you!

Knock, knock...
Who's there?
Butter...
Butter who?
Butter bring an
umbrella!

Knock, knock...
Who's there?
Darwin...
Darwin who?
I'll be Darwin you
open the door!

☺☺☺☺☺ ☺☺☺☺☺

Knock, knock...
Who's there?
Bella...
Bella who?
Bella bottom
trousers!

Knock, knock...
Who's there?
Guess Simon...
Guess Simon who?
Guess Simon the wrong doorstep!

Knock, knock...
Who's there?
Hedda...
Hedda who?
Hedda nough of this – I'm off!

Knock, knock...
Who's there?
Cugat...
Cugat who?
Cugat to love my jokes!

Knock, knock...
Who's there?
Curry...
Curry who?
Curry me back home will you!

Knock, knock...
Who's there?
Cynthia...
Cynthia who?
Cynthia you been away I missed you!

Knock, knock...
Who's there?
Barbara...
Barbara who?
Barbara
black sheep,
have you any
wool...?

Knock, knock...
Who's there?
Eva...
Eva who?
Eva you're deaf or your doorbell isn't working!

☺☺☺☺☺ ☺☺☺☺☺

Knock, knock...
Who's there?
Ears...
Ears who?
Ears looking at you!

Knock, knock...
Who's there?
Earl...
Earl who?
Earl be glad to tell you
when you open this door!

Knock, knock...
Who's there?
Eddie...
Eddie who?
Eddie body home?

Knock, knock...
Who's there?
Edith...
Edith who?
Edith, it'll make you feel better!

Knock, knock...
Who's there?
Perth...
Perth who?
Perth your lips and whistle!

Knock, knock...
Who's there?
Ella Man...
Ella Man who?
Ella Man-tary my dear Watson!

Knock, knock...
Who's there?
Elsie...
Elsie who?
Elsie you around!

Knock, knock...
Who's there?
Ferrer...
Ferrer who?
Ferrer'vrything there is a season!

Knock, knock...
Who's there?
Eugenie...
Eugenie who?
Eugenie from the bottle
who will grant me
three wishes?

Knock, knock...
Who's there?
Datsun...
Datsun who?
Datsun old joke!

Knock, knock...
Who's there?
Dawn...
Dawn who?
Dawn leave me out here in the cold!

Knock, knock...
Who's there?
Emma...
Emma who?
Emma bit cold out here, can you let me in?

☺☺☺☺☺ ☺☺☺☺☺

Knock, knock...
Who's there?
Emmett...
Emmett who?
Emmett your service!

Knock, knock...
Who's there?
Annie...
Annie who?
Annie one you like!

Knock, knock...
Who's there?
Conyers...
Conyers who?
Conyers please open
the door!

Knock, knock...
Who's there?
Woody...
Woody who?
Woody open the door if
we ask him nicely?

☺☺☺☺☺ ☺☺☺☺☺

Knock, knock...
Who's there?
Galway...
Galway who?
Galway, your
annoying me!

Knock, knock...
Who's there?
Denis...
Denis who?
Denis anyone?

Knock, knock...
Who's there?
Denise...
Denise who?
Denise are above your ankles!

Knock, knock...
Who's there?
Deanna...
Deanna who?
Deanna-mals are restless, open the cage!

Knock, knock...
Who's there?
Deena...
Deena who?
Deena hear me the first time?

Knock, knock...
Who's there?
Watson...
Watson who?
Watson TV tonight?

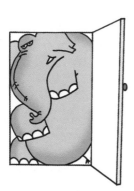

Knock, knock...
Who's there?
Haydn...
Haydn who?
Haydn in this cupboard
is boring!

Knock, knock...
Who's there?
Delores...
Delores who?
Delores is on the side of the good guys!

☺☺☺☺☺ ☺☺☺☺☺

Knock, knock...
Who's there?
Bernadette...
Bernadette who?
Bernadette all my dinner and now I'm starving!

Knock, knock...
Who's there?
Glasgow...
Glasgow who?
Glasgow to the movies!

Knock, knock...
Who's there?
Godunov...
Godunov who?
Godunov to eat!

Knock, knock...
Who's there?
Egbert...
Egbert who?
Egbert no bacon!

Knock, knock...
Who's there?
Yootha...
Yootha who?
Yootha person with the second hand
cooker for sale?

Knock, knock...
Who's there?
Diesel...
Diesel who?
Diesel teach me to go knocking
around on
doors!

Knock, knock...
Who's there?
Chicken...
Chicken who?
Chicken the oven, I
can smell burning!

Knock, knock...
Who's there?
Hyman...
Hyman who?
Hyman in the mood for dancing...!

☺☺☺☺☺ ☺☺☺☺☺

Knock, knock...
Who's there?
Grant...
Grant who?
Grant you a wish,
what is it?

Knock, knock...
Who's there?
Ethan...
Ethan who?
Ethan me out of house and home you are!

Knock, knock...
Who's there?
Essen...
Essen who?
Essen it fun to listen to these jokes?

Knock, knock...
Who's there?
Goose...
Goose who?
Goose see a doctor, you don't look well!

  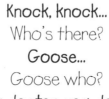

Knock, knock...
Who's there?
Gopher...
Gopher who?
Gopher broke!

Knock, knock...
Who's there?
Chile...
Chile who?
Chile out tonight isn't it?

Knock, knock...
Who's there?
Disguise...
Disguise who?
Disguise the limit!

Knock, knock...
Who's there?
Gladys...
Gladys who?
Gladys the weekend, aren't you?

Knock, knock...
Who's there?
Herman...
Herman who?
Herman is handsome!

Knock, knock...
Who's there?
Figs...
Figs who?
Figs the doorbell, it's broken!

Knock, knock...
Who's there?
Florinda...
Florinda who?
Florinda bathroom is wet!

Knock, knock...
Who's there?
Dimension...
Dimension who?
Dimension it!

Knock, knock...
Who's there?
Dinah...
Dinah who?
**Dinah shoot until you see
the whites of their eyes!**

KNOCK KNOCK JOKES

Knock, knock...
Who's there?
Gable...
Gable who?
Gable to leap buildings in a single bound!

Knock, knock...
Who's there?
Heart...
Heart who?
Heart to hear you,
speak up!

Knock, knock...
Who's there?
Harry...
Harry who?
Harry you been?

☺☺☺☺☺ ☺☺☺☺☺

Knock, knock...
Who's there?
Jean...
Jean who?
Jeanius - you just
don't know it!

Knock, knock...
Who's there?
Denver...
Denver who?
Denver the good old days?

Knock, knock...
Who's there?
Desi...
Desi who?
Desi'gnated hitter!

Knock, knock...
Who's there?
Gravy...
Gravy who?
Gravy Crockett!

Knock, knock...
Who's there?
Greta...
Greta who?
You Greta on my nerves!

Knock, knock...
Who's there?
Haiti...
Haiti who?
Haiti see a good thing go to waste!

Knock, knock...
Who's there?
Irma...
Irma who?
Irma big girl now!

Knock, knock...
Who's there?
Gordie...
Gordie who?
Gordie-rectly to jail, do not pass go,
do not collect £200!

Knock, knock...
Who's there?
Hugo...
Hugo who?
Hugo your way
and I'll go mine!

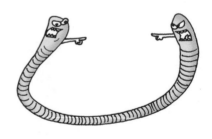

Knock, knock...
Who's there?
Dino...
Dino who?
Dino the answer?

Knock, knock...
Who's there?
Disaster...
Disaster who?
Disaster be my lucky day!

 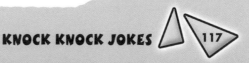

Knock, knock...
Who's there?
Guinevere...
Guinevere who?
Guinevere going to get together?

Knock, knock...
Who's there?
Haifa...
Haifa who?
Haifa cake is better than none!

Knock, knock...
Who's there?
Hair...
Hair who?
Hair today, gone tomorrow!

Knock, knock...
Who's there?
Iona...
Iona who?
Iona a great
train set!

Knock, knock...
Who's there?
Ivory...
Ivory who?
Ivory strong, just like Tarzan!

Knock, knock...
Who's there?
Hanover...
Hanover who?
Hanover your money!

Knock, knock...
Who's there?
Disk...
Disk who?
Disk is recorded message, please leave your
message after the beep!

Knock, knock...
Who's there?
Don...
Don who?
Don Patrol!

Knock, knock...
Who's there?
Pizza...
Pizza who?
Pizza the pie!

Knock, knock...
Who's there?
Halifax...
Halifax who?
Halifax you if you fax me!

Knock, knock...
Who's there?
Harriet...
Harriet who?
Harriet it up!

Knock, knock...
Who's there?
Jaws...
Jaws who?
Jaws truly!

Knock, knock...
Who's there?
Dishes...
Dishes who?
Dishes a very bad joke!

☺☺☺☺☺ ☺☺☺☺☺

Knock, knock...
Who's there?
Colin...
Colin who?
Colin all cars,
Colin all cars!

Knock, knock...
Who's there?
Fozzie...
Fozzie who?
Fozzie hundredth time let me in!

Knock, knock...
Who's there?
Freddie...
Freddie who?
Freddie or not here I come!

Knock, knock...
Who's there?
Freighter...
Freighter who?
I'm Freighter open the door!

Knock, knock...
Who's there?
Fresno...
Fresno who?
Rudolf the Fresno reindeer...!

Knock, knock...
Who's there?
Fez...
Fez who?
Fez me, that's who!

☺☺☺☺☺  ☺☺☺☺☺

Knock, knock...
Who's there?
Felix...
Felix who?
Felix my ice cream, I'll
lick his!

Knock, knock...
Who's there?
Genoa...
Genoa who?
Genoa any new jokes?

☺☺☺☺☺ ☺☺☺☺☺

Knock, knock...
Who's there?
Giza...
Giza who?
Giza nice boy!